STEM *trailblazer* BIOS

ENVIRONMENTAL
ACTIVIST
WANGARI MAATHAI

JENNIFER SWANSON

Lerner Publications ◆ Minneapolis

Wangari Maathai's love for nature helped spark a worldwide environmental movement.

CONNECTING WITH
THE LAND

Among the green trees and wide plains of Kenya, Wangari Maathai was born on April 1, 1940. She went on to do amazing things for her country and her people. She became the first woman in central and East Africa to earn an advanced college degree. Maathai was a big supporter of women's rights and worked for the equal treatment of women throughout her life. She also led the Green Belt Movement, one of the largest environmental revolutions in Africa. In 2004, Maathai was recognized for her achievements with a Nobel Peace Prize. She was the first African woman to ever receive the honor.

Maathai shakes hands with Ole Mjoes, chairman of the Nobel Prize committee.

Maathai was a member of the Kikuyu, the largest ethnic group in Kenya. She was born during the rainy season in the tiny village of Ihithe. Rain filled the streams and lakes. It gave life to the trees, the animals, and the people. Maathai's love of nature and her determination to help others would make her a world-famous activist and voice for the environment.

A Kikuyu mother and son pose for a photo in front of their home. Kenya is home to millions of Kikuyu.

EARLY YEARS

Wangari was the third of six children and the oldest girl. Her father was a tenant farmer. He grew crops and sold them to the British owner of the land. The landowner earned much more money than Wangari's father did. Still, her father loved the land he tended. Wangari loved it too.

Wangari spent the first few years of her life like many young Kenyan girls. She helped her mother take care of Wangari's younger sisters and did other chores. Wangari noticed everything, especially the trees. She knew the bushes, the streams, and the animals.

TENANT FARMING

Tenant farmers grow crops and tend land they do not own. Tenant farmers were common in Africa in the mid-twentieth century. Kenya was controlled then by Britain. After World War I (1914–1918), the British government gave many wealthy British people land in Kenya. The new landowners hired tenant farmers to work the land.

A WONDERFUL OPPORTUNITY

When Wangari was seven years old, she and her mother moved to Nyeri, Kenya, where Wangari's older brothers were going to school. She was supposed to help her mother fix meals for the family and do other household chores.

In the 1940s, it was unusual for girls in Kenya to go to school. Most worked with their mothers around the home. But Wangari wanted to go to school too. She had questions about everything. She was mainly interested in plants and animals. Wangari had her own garden where she grew corn and beans. She would watch butterflies and bees buzzing around her crops. She longed to know more about the ways plants, animals, and people interacted and relied on one another.

One of Wangari's brothers understood that she had many questions. He urged her to go to school, and their mother agreed. So at eight years of age, Wangari began the daily 3-mile (4.8 km) trek to school. She didn't mind the long walk. She hoped that school would help her learn more about nature and how things grow.

Farms that grow coffee beans are an important part of Nyeri's economy.

Chapter 2

President John F. Kennedy supported bringing Kenyan students to the United States with the help of the Joseph P. Kennedy Jr. Foundation.

FINDING ROOTS IN EDUCATION

Maathai loved learning and did well in school. She graduated from high school in 1959 near the top of her class. Her good grades made it possible to receive a special honor. In 1960, Maathai received a **scholarship** from the

Joseph P. Kennedy Jr. Foundation. It would allow her to attend college in the United States.

Maathai spent the next several years earning a bachelor's degree in biology from Mount Saint Scholastica in Atchison, Kansas. She went on to get her master's degree in biology from the University of Pittsburgh. Maathai's research focused on how the pineal gland, a tiny organ in the brain, works. She studied Japanese quail to see how the pineal gland develops during the bird's life. She learned to raise quail from eggs and observe their growth to adulthood.

The University of Pittsburgh was founded in 1787 and has many grand, historic buildings.

Maathai's time in the United States had been rewarding, but she longed to go back home. She returned to Kenya in 1966. Big changes had taken place while she was gone. The country had gained its independence from Britain. The people of Kenya were finally free to control their own government and future. Maathai wanted to be part of it.

CHALLENGING WOMEN'S ROLES

In the United States in the 1960s, women had begun to enjoy many of the same freedoms and opportunities as men. But things were different in Kenya. Women were still expected to fill traditional roles such as housekeeping and gathering crops. They very rarely got jobs outside the home or went to college.

Maathai hadn't returned to Kenya to fill a traditional role.

In 1971, she made history by graduating from the University of Nairobi's School of Veterinary Medicine. She was the first woman to earn the rank of doctor in central or East Africa. Her determination to earn an advanced degree despite the expectations of her community had served Maathai well.

MAKING PROGRESS

Shortly after graduation, Maathai became the first female professor at the University of Nairobi. Working at the university was an honor, but Maathai was unhappy with how women on the school's staff were treated. They did not receive the same salary and housing benefits as the men. Maathai gathered a group of female employees, and together, they demanded equal treatment. The university leaders took notice. They agreed to some of the group's demands.

Maathai's first taste of political action had been a success. The experience taught her that too often people took advantage of women based solely on their gender. Maathai knew that women were equal to men, and she wanted to help women in Kenya fight to prove it.

Chapter 3

Maathai knew that it takes a long time for trees to grow and that people could destroy forests quickly.

PLANTING FOR THE FUTURE

After her successful effort to gain equal treatment for women at the university, Maathai wanted to continue working for causes she believed in. She turned her attention to the environment.

Deforestation had become a problem in Kenya. People had cut down huge forests to make more land available for farming and houses. Without trees for shade, the soil became dry. Water dried up quickly in the sun. Kenya's rich soil was being eroded, or swept away, without trees to protect it from the wind and rain. Crops couldn't grow without the rich soil Maathai remembered from her youth. The country was suffering, and so were its people.

People cut down trees to use as fuel and to make way for buildings and roads.

TECH TALK

"It's the little things citizens do. That's what will make the difference. My little thing is planting trees."

—*Wangari Maathai*

The answer to deforestation was simple, at least in theory. Start planting new trees. But the government did not have a

program to replace trees that had been cut down. For many years in Kenya, more trees had been destroyed than were replanted. Maathai set out to change that.

Maathai observed that many people didn't understand the importance of trees. If forests were to make a comeback in Kenya, she would have to help educate people.

DEFORESTATION HARMS ANIMALS

Forests are extremely important animal habitats. Animals use trees for food and shelter. Without trees, animals face greater threats from predators, as well as exposure to wind, rain, and natural disasters. As forests disappear, animals must make dangerous journeys across roads and travel around fenced fields to reach new habitats. Some animals rely on certain types of trees that may be rare. Destroying those trees puts animal populations in danger.

Chapter 4

Many people in Kenya rely on charcoal to cook and heat their homes. Most of the charcoal is made from trees.

TAKING ACTION

In the early 1970s, Maathai searched for a solution to Kenya's deforestation. She began in **rural** areas that were suffering the most from missing forests. She spoke with women living in small villages like Ihithe, where Maathai was born. She saw their problems caused by fewer trees. Fresh, clean water was hard to find. The people lacked firewood for cooking and warmth. Food was becoming hard to grow as the ground dried. To survive and provide for their families, these women walked long distances every day to find fresh water and firewood. Maathai knew what she had to do.

People may burn forests to clear land quickly.

THE GREEN BELT MOVEMENT

Maathai began a massive **reforestation** program called the Green Belt Movement in 1977. She involved women living in rural villages. She taught them how to plant trees with the goal of reforesting Kenya. They started small, growing **seedlings** in a nursery. As the trees grew, they were replanted throughout the country.

The Green Belt Movement got its name from the long lines, or belts, of trees that the group planted.

Maathai didn't just talk about planting trees. She often helped plant trees herself.

Maathai got help from women all around Kenya. The Green Belt Movement paid them for every tree they planted. Not only did the program help plant millions of trees, but it also brought money to the villages. The people had fresh water and firewood again, and the money helped families grow and thrive.

CONFLICT WITH LEADERS

Not everyone supported the Green Belt Movement. Maathai knew that the leaders of the Kenyan government made money from deforestation by erecting buildings on cleared land. They wanted her to stop planting trees and educating people about the dangers of forest loss. Maathai refused. She was threatened, and several times, she was arrested and physically injured.

The Green Belt Movement planted trees in nurseries such as this one before replanting the trees all around the country.

Maathai continued to speak out. She encouraged all Kenyans to be proud of their country and protect its environment. She spoke directly to the women of Kenya. She asked them to become leaders in their communities and protect the land. She said they should stand up against injustice and work to make Kenya a better place.

Maathai displays a handful of rich Kenyan soil.

TECH TALK

"We have planted over 30 million trees that provide fuel, food, shelter, and income to support their children's education and household needs. The activity also creates employment and improves soils."

—*Wangari Maathai*

Chapter 5

Maathai gives a speech during her campaign to be elected to the Kenyan government.

INSPIRING A GENERATION

In 2002, Maathai was elected to the Kenyan government. She was named deputy minister for the environment. She continued to fight for the plants, animals, and people of Kenya.

Two years later, Maathai was recognized for her ongoing **humanitarian** work. She was awarded one of the most famous honors in the world: the Nobel Peace Prize.

President Mwai Kibaki of Kenya offers Maathai a congratulatory handshake in 2004 for winning the Nobel Peace Prize.

GREEN PLANET

According to one estimate, more than three trillion trees are on Earth. But every year about fifteen million trees are cut down. This greatly affects the climate, as trees give off oxygen and absorb gases that warm the planet. Tree-planting programs such as the Green Belt Movement are working to make sure Earth has enough trees.

This satellite image shows brown areas where humans have cleared away large portions of forests.

Maathai *(right)* plants a tree with US president Barack Obama in 2006.

Maathai was the first African woman to receive a Nobel Peace Prize. Her dedication to the environment and concern for African women had paid off. The Green Belt Movement planted millions of trees and empowered thousands of Kenyan women. In the words of the Nobel Peace Prize committee, "[Maathai] thinks globally and acts locally."

ROOTED IN SUCCESS

Maathai died in 2011 after a battle with cancer. But her legacy lives on. The Green Belt Movement has planted more than fifty-one million trees in Kenya and has helped countless women. Maathai's efforts have inspired other environmental groups as well. Organizations have sprung up around the world because of her example. They are all interested in keeping Earth healthy. Some support clean water. Others are interested in combating climate change. And, of course, there are programs that focus on planting trees. Maathai's determination and love of nature inspired these groups, just as the trees and the land inspired her.

TECH TALK

"We owe it to ourselves and to the next generation to conserve the environment so that we can [leave] our children a sustainable world that benefits all."

—*Wangari Maathai*

TIMELINE

1940

Wangari Maathai is born in Ihithe, a small village in Kenya.

1960

Maathai wins a scholarship and goes to the United States to study biology.

1971

Maathai becomes the first woman in central and East Africa to earn the title of doctor.

1977

Maathai starts the Green Belt Movement to reforest Kenya and provide jobs for women.

2002

Maathai is elected to Kenya's government and serves as deputy minister for the environment.

2004

Maathai is awarded the Nobel Peace Prize for her contributions to the environment, democracy, and peace in Africa.

2009

Maathai becomes a United Nations Messenger of Peace, focusing on the environment and climate change.

2011

Maathai dies in Nairobi, Kenya.

SOURCE NOTES

7 Wangari Maathai, *Unbowed: A Memoir* (New York: Anchor Books, 2007), 45.

12 Ibid., 138.

16 "Words to Live By—a Tribute to Wangari Maathai," Project Learning Tree, accessed March 10, 2017, https://www.plt.org/educator-tips/words-to-live-by -tribute-wangari-maathai.

23 Wangari Maathai, "Nobel Lecture," Nobelprize.org, December 10, 2004, http:// www.nobelprize.org/nobel_prizes/peace/laureates/2004/maathai-lecture -text.html.

27 "The Nobel Peace Prize," Green Belt Movement, accessed March 10, 2017, http://www.greenbeltmovement.org/wangari-maathai/the-nobel-peace-prize.

28 Joseph Kabiru, "Farewell Wangari Maathai, You Were a Global Inspiration— and My Heroine, *Guardian* (US ed.), September 26, 2011, https://www .theguardian.com/global-development/poverty-matters/2011/sep/26 /farewell-wangari-maathai-my-heroine.

GLOSSARY

deforestation
the process of cutting down or clearing forests

humanitarian
work to improve the lives of other people

reforestation
planting trees to create new forests

rural
in the countryside, not near a city

scholarship
money awarded to a student to pay for school

seedlings
young plants that have just sprouted from seeds

FURTHER INFORMATION

BOOKS

Cornell, Kari. *Urban Biologist Danielle Lee*. Minneapolis: Lerner Publications, 2016. Wish you could learn more about what biologists do? Read this book about Danielle Lee.

Hustad, Douglas. *Animal Scientist and Activist Jane Goodall*. Minneapolis: Lerner Publications, 2017. Find out how Jane Goodall pursued her passion for animals and helped scientists understand their behavior.

Kalman, Bobbie. *Spotlight on Kenya*. New York: Crabtree, 2013. Read more about the wildlife, land, and people of Kenya.

WEBSITES

Kids for a Clean Environment
http://www.kidsface.org
Learn about kids around the world who are making a difference in their environment by planting trees, recycling, and keeping things clean.

Plant a Tree
https://education.usgs.gov/kids/plantatree.html
This US government website has detailed instructions for planting trees.

Science for Kids
http://www.scienceforkidsclub.com
Check out this website for more information about a wide range of science topics.

Expand learning beyond the printed book. Download free, complementary educational resources for this book from our website, www.lerneresource.com.

INDEX

Britain, 8, 12

college, 5, 11–13

deforestation, 15–18, 22

deputy minister for the environment, 24

government, 12, 16, 22, 24

Green Belt Movement, 5, 20–22, 26–28

habitat, 17

Ihithe, Kenya, 6, 18

Joseph P. Kennedy Jr. Foundation, 10–11

Kikuyu, 6

Mount Saint Scholastica, 11

Nobel Peace Prize, 5, 25, 27

Nyeri, Kenya, 8

reforestation, 20

scholarship, 10

school, 8–11, 13

tenant farmer, 7–8

University of Nairobi, 13

University of Pittsburgh, 11

ABOUT THE AUTHOR

Jennifer Swanson is the author of more than twenty-five STEM books for kids. She is always thrilled to learn about pioneering women who have helped the world through their love of science.